Pub Grub

Authentic British Pub Food Recipes

Giles M. L. Hawkins

Copyright
Giles M. L. Hawkins
2008

Introduction

British food suffers, unjustly, from a terrible reputation. People often think of British food as being bland, poorly cooked, and greasy. However, this is largely due to the places visitors have encountered food in Britain. Real British food has a long heritage and many different influences. Unfortunately, visitors to Britain do not often find typically British food, particularly in England. Ireland, Scotland and Wales have done a better job of preserving their national foods. England has become a great melting pot of cultures and its native foods have suffered. It is now quite difficult to find the foods on the following pages in pubs and restaurants as they have been displaced by frozen and reheated substitutions or things appearing under the same names, but poor immitations. Perhaps even worse are the plethora of mediocre curries, kebabs, and a substance that masquerades as Chile Con Carne. Good, and even great food is still available in homes, but the visitor rarely gets to sample those.

This book then is at least a peek into the great food of yesteryear's pubs and inns. It is substantial, tasty and warming. It is designed to be eaten with real British Ales to fully enjoy the experience. *A note about beer: Real British beer is pulled from casks, not pushed by carbonation to your glass. It is not served, as many believe, warm. Beer is served at 'cellar temperature', which is somewhere about 54 - 57°F. It is cold, but never icy. The cooler the beer, the less flavor it has. Ale is brown to dark brown in color, should be ever so slightly effervescent, and have a nice head on it when poured. These are considered, proudly by the British as 'real beer'. Lagers and Pilsners, however pleasant they may occasionally be are not 'real beer'. Many American package stores now have a good selection of British Ales in cans and bottles.*

The recipes herein are authentic (although they have been carefully tailored to be prepared in America). Many of the recipes are family recipes or have been culled from antique cookbooks, and each of them has been prepared by the author – or the author's family. These are the authentic tastes of Britain and great British pubs and inns. These recipes can serve as a slice of home to expatriate Brits, and an introduction to curious and Anglophile Americans.

Table of Contents

Tracklements   5

Main Courses   13

Side Dishes   37

Puddings   49

The Basics   59

Index   65

Tracklements

Recipes

Branford Relish 7

Green Tomato Chutney 8

Piccalilli 9

Pickled Onions 10

Salad Cream 11

Branford Relish

Known by another, but similar name commercially.

9 ounces carrots, peeled and cut into small chunks
1 medium rutabaga, peeled and cut into small chunks
4-5 garlic cloves, peeled and finely chopped
5 ounces dates, finely chopped
1 small cauliflower, finely chopped
2 onions, peeled and finely chopped
2 medium apples, finely chopped, unpeeled
2 medium finely chopped zucchini, unpeeled
15-20 small Cornichons finely chopped
1⅔ cups brown sugar
1 tsp sea salt
4 tbsp lemon juice
16 ounces cider vinegar
2 tsp mustard seeds
2 tsp ground allspice
1 tsp cayenne pepper

Combine all the ingredients in a large saucepan and bring them to the boil. Reduce the heat to a simmer and cook until the rutabaga is cooked, but remains firm, about 2 hours. Stir well to redistribute all of the vegetables. Bottle and seal in sterile and hot jars. Allow the pickle to age for a few weeks before using. This improves the taste and it will become more "mellow".

Green Tomato Chutney

2 lbs green tomatoes
1 lb green apples
½ lb shallots
6 cloves garlic
¾ lb brown sugar
1 lb golden raisins
1½ tsp salt
½ tsp cayenne pepper
½ tsp ground ginger
½ tsp ground cardamom
½ tsp ground cinnamon
2 cups apple cider vinegar

Chop all vegetables. Place all ingredients in a large pot, stirring in the vinegar. Cook until the mixture is dark and thick – about 1 hour. Allow to cool and bottle in glass jars.

Piccalilli

2 lbs cauliflower, cut into small pieces
2 lbs cucumber, peeled and diced
2 lbs zucchini, peeled and diced
2 lbs pearl onions
⅛ Cup turmeric
¼-cup English mustard (prepared)
¼-cup sugar
2 tbsp corn flour
Cider vinegar
Pickling spice

Place vegetables in a large pot and sprinkle with salt. Leave for 12 hours.

Add vinegar to the pot to cover the vegetables and 2 oz pickling spice in a bag. Bring to a boil and boil for 10 minutes.

Combine turmeric, mustard powder, sugar, and corn flour. Mix in enough cold vinegar to make a runny, smooth paste. Add to vegetables, stir in well and boil for a further 10 minutes. Allow to cool and bottle.

Pickled Onions

7 lbs small white onions
1-cup pickling salt
2 quarts cider vinegar
½-cup sugar
4 tsp mustard seeds
8 bay leaves

Peel and par boil the onions for two minutes. Place the onions in a large bowl and cover with cold water. Add pickling salt and stir to dissolve. Let stand at room temperature for 24 hours.

Wash and dry 8 (1-pint) jars and lids. Stand on a baking sheet and keep warm in a 250°F oven.

Rinse onions under running water and drain well. Bring vinegar, sugar, and spices to a boil in a non-reactive pan, stirring occasionally.

Meanwhile, pack jars with onions and then pour the boiling vinegar into the jars leaving about half an inch at the top, distributing the mustard seeds and bay leaves evenly. Wipe the rims and seal the jars. Cool and store in a cool, dark place. Let stand 1 week before using.

Serve with pork pie, pasties, and sandwiches.

Salad Cream

1 tbsp prepared English mustard
1 tbsp plain flour
2 eggs
Cream
1 tbsp sugar
½ tsp salt
½-cup vinegar

Mix mustard, sugar, flour, and salt together. Add the eggs, then vinegar. Stand in boiling water and stir until mixture thickens. Allow it to get quite cold. Add cream, whisking until the mixture is the required thickness. It should be the consistency of Thousand Island dressing.

Main Courses

Recipes

Cheshire Pork and Apple Pie	15
Beef in Guinness	16
Cornish Pasties	17
Farmhouse Pie	18
Fish and Chips	19
Gammon Steaks	20
Pork Pie	21
Roast Beef	23
Sausage Rolls	24
Scotch Eggs	25
Steak and Ale Pie	26
Steak and Kidney Pie	27
Toad in the Hole	28
Welsh Rarebit	29
Beef Olives	30
Beef Croquettes	31
Ploughman's Lunch	32
Shepherd's Pie *and Cottage Pie*	33
Fisherman's Pie	34
Bangers and Mash	35

Cheshire Pork and Apple Pie

1 batch of shortcrust pastry

1 lb lean pork
1 lb fatty pork
3 strip of bacon
1½ lbs granny smith apples
1 large yellow onion chopped
2 oz butter
5 oz light ale
Rubbed sage
Nutmeg
Salt
Pepper

Preheat the oven to 350°F.

Grind the pork (or chop to a very fine dice) and the bacon. Chop the onion to a fine dice. Mix the meat and the onion together and season with salt, pepper, and sage. Peel, core and slice the apples; season them with sugar and nutmeg.

Line a pie dish with pastry, and trim the edge. Put a layer of meat into the pie dish and then a layer of apples, then pork, then apples. Dot with butter on top and pour in the ale. Top the pie with a disk of pastry, crimping the edge. Cut a vent in the top and glaze the pic with an egg wash.

Bake the pie for 1¼ hours. The pie may be eaten hot or cold.

Beef in Guinness

2½ lb of stew beef
2 large onions
6 medium carrots
2 tbsp seasoned flour
a little fat or beef dripping
½ cup dry cider (the alcoholic sort)
1½ cup Guinness with water
sprig of parsley

Cut the beef into chunks, peel, and slice the onions and carrots. Toss the beef in the flour and brown quickly in hot fat. Remove the beef and fry the onions gently until transparent. Return the beef and add the carrots and the liquid. Bring just to the boil, reduce the heat to a very gentle simmer, cover closely and cook for 1½ - 2 hours. Check that the dish does not dry out, adding more liquid if necessary. Sprinkle with chopped parsley and serve with plainly boiled potatoes.

Cornish Pasties

Filling
1 cup cooked cubed beef.
1 small potato, peeled, diced
1 small carrot, peeled, thinly sliced
1 medium onion, finely chopped
5oz gravy
1 tbsp steak sauce.
¼ tsp each, salt & pepper

Pastry
4 cups sifted flour
2 tsp salt
1½ cups chilled shortening
½ cup of ice water
1 egg yoke beaten with 1 tbsp of cold water

Mix flour and salt in large bowl and cut in shortening with a pastry blender until the texture of oatmeal. Sprinkle water over surface a tablespoonful at a time, mixing with a fork after each addition. Pastry should just hold together. Wrap in foil and rest in refrigerator while preparing filling.

Mix all filling ingredients.

Roll out 6-6 ½" pastry circles.
Divide filling among circles.
Brush edges with egg wash to seal.
For each pastry, bring up two sides above filling and pinch together,
Crimping to make a wavy edge.
Place on a lightly greased baking tray.
Brush all over top with egg wash.
Bake in 425° oven for 15 min, reducing heat to 350° for 30min.
Can be served hot or cold.

Farmhouse Pie

Filling
1½ lbs beef chuck
½ cup flour
1 tsp salt
3 medium sized potatoes
1 large yellow onion
1 ⅔ cups rich beef stock
½ tsp dried thyme
Pepper

Pastry
2 cups sifted flour
1 tsp salt
⅓ cup chilled shortening
⅓ cup chilled lard
4-5 tsp ice water
1 egg yolk mixed with 1 tbsp cold water

Peel and slice the potatoes into ½" thick slices. Cube the beef into 1" cubes. Peel and slice the onion into thin slices.

Preheat oven to 425ºF. Prepare the pastry:- Sift the flour and the salt into a bowl, and cut in the shortening and lard with a pastry blender until it is the texture of oatmeal. Sprinkle ice water over surface a tbsp at a time, mixing with a fork after each addition. The pastry should just hold together. Wrap in foil and place in the refrigerator while you make the beef filling. Dredge the beef in flour and salt. Put the beef with all the salt and the flour, and the thyme into the bottom of a 1½ quart casserole with a wide rim. Layer the potatoes and onion on top of the beef with salt and pepper between all the layers. Pour the stock over all. Roll the pastry into a circle about 3 inches larger than the casserole. Cut a strip from the outside of the circle. Moisten the rim of the casserole with water and place the strip on the moistened rim. Moisten strip and place the circle of pastry over the filling. Trim the pastry around the edges of the casserole and crimp down the edges to seal. Make a hole in the center of the pie to vent. Brush the top of the pie with the egg wash, avoiding the edge. Bake 15 minutes and reduce the temperature to 350ºF and bake a further 1¼ hours till the meat is tender (test through the hole in the center).

Serve with vegetables and gravy.

Fish and Chips

Vegetable oil
3 large potatoes
2 cups rice flour
1 tbsp baking powder
3 tbsp salt
12 oz club soda
1 large egg, lightly beaten
2 (8-ounce) cod or haddock fillets, cut in half
½ cup rice flour, for dredging

Heat 3 inches of the oil in a deep fryer (alternatively use a deep, heavy skillet) to 325 degrees F.

Peel the potatoes and cut them into chips about the size of your index finger. Put the potatoes in a fryer basket and lower into the oil. Fry the chips for 2 to 3 minutes; they should not be crisp or fully cooked at this point. Remove the chips to a paper towel-lined platter to drain.

Crank the oil temperature up to 375 degrees F. In a large mixing bowl, combine the flour, baking powder, salt, and pepper. Combine soda water and egg and pour into the flour mixture. Whisk to a smooth batter. Spread the rice flour on a plate. Dredge the fish pieces in the rice flour and then dip them into the batter, letting the excess drip off.

Put the chips in the bottom of the fryer basket and carefully submerge in the hot oil. Carefully lower the battered fish into the bubbling oil on top of the chips. Fry the fish and chips for 4 to 5 minutes until crispy and brown. Remove the basket and drain the fish and chips on paper towels; season lightly with salt.

Serve with malt vinegar.

Gammon Steaks

Gammon is an old English term that refers to the ham or hind leg of a pig. References date to as early as the year 1482 in literature.

4 - ½ inch slices of cooked ham.
4 slices of pineapple

Arrange slices of ham on a baking sheet. Broil ham steak on each side until lightly browned. Place a ring of pineapple on each slice of ham and broil until the pineapple is heated through.

Serve with peas and chips.

Pork Pie

1 lb plain flour
1 egg yolk
6 oz lard, diced
⅔ cup water
2 tbsp confectioner's sugar
2 lbs lean pork cut into ¼ inch dice
3 strips of meaty bacon, finely diced

2 tsp dried sage
2 tsp dried thyme
2 tsp anchovy paste
½ tsp ground nutmeg
½ tsp ground allspice
20 oz chicken stock
1 egg, beaten with 1 tbsp water (to glaze)
½ oz gelatin powder

Warm a mixing bowl and sieve the flour and confectioner's sugar into it. Make a well in the center and add the egg yolk. Gently heat the lard in the water until it has melted, and then bring rapidly to a boil. Pour immediately into the well in the flour and draw the ingredients together with a wooden spoon to form a soft, pliable, but not sticky ball of dough. Transfer to a lightly floured surface and knead until it is smooth and elastic with no cracks. Cover and leave to rest in a warm place for 20-30 minutes. Preheat the oven to 400°F.

Mix the pork, bacon, herbs, anchovy, and spices. Moisten with three tbsp of the stock.

Roll out two thirds of the pastry on a lightly floured surface and line a raised pie mould or spring form pan. Pack the meat mixture into the pastry. Roll out the remaining pastry to make a lid for the pie. Press the edges together tightly to seal. Scallop the edges and decorate with pastry leaves. Cut a hole in the centre of the lid. Brush the top with beaten egg. Place on a baking sheet. Bake for 20 minutes. Reduce the temperature to 350°F and bake for a further 2 ¼ hours. Remove the mould, brush the sides and top with egg glaze and return to the oven for 10-15 minutes, until well browned. Remove from the oven, leave until room temperature.

Heat the stock in a saucepan and sprinkle in the gelatin. Stir briskly until dissolved. Leave to cool, but not set. Pour liquid through the hole in the pastry lid. Leave in a cool place overnight. Serve cut in thick slices.

For lunch, serve with a salad of lettuce, tomatoes, and salad cream; pickled onions; piccalilli; and cheese.

For dinner, serve with baked beans, and chips

Roast Beef

The British are so fond of roast beef that the French refer to us as 'Les Rosbifs'. Accompanied by real gravy, roast potatoes, brussel sprouts, parsnips, and Yorkshire pudding, this meal will grace Sunday lunch tables the length and breadth of Britain every week.

A rib of beef roast on the bone, weighing about 4-5 lb
1 tbsp English mustard
Freshly ground black pepper
Coarse salt
2 tbsp plain flour
10oz beef stock

Preheat the oven to 475F, or as high as it will go. Rub the fat side of the meat with mustard and a couple of generous pinches of salt. Put the meat in a roasting tin, resting on the bones, with the fat side up. Roast the meat for 15 minutes, and then reduce the heat to 350F. Roast for 10 minutes/lb for rare meat, 15 minutes/lb for medium, 20 minutes/lb for well done, basting every half hour or so with the dripping in the pan. (If your roast is boneless, then rest it on a rack and cook it for 2 minutes/lb less.

Take the meat out and leave in a warm place for at least 15 minutes or up to an hour.

For the gravy, pour most of the fat out of the roasting tin (use it for the Yorkshire puddings) leaving only a tablespoonful or so behind. Put the roasting pan on the range top over a medium heat. Whisk the flour into the pan juices, and stir until the mixture becomes a light golden color. Remove the pan from the heat, and pour in the stock gradually, stirring vigorously, – If the liquid is added too fast or while still on the heat and you will risk lumps - and scraping up the fond from the base of the pan. Simmer for 10 minutes or so, adding extra water or stock if necessary. Adjust the seasoning to taste.

Sausage Rolls

1 lb sage sausage meat
1 package flaky pastry
1 egg

Preheat the oven to 400°F. Flatten out the pastry onto a floured board. Cut the pastry into nine equal squares, slicing three strips along the folds, and then each strip.

Divide the sausage into 18 equal portions. Form a roll of the sausage meat to fit in each of the pastry squares. Roll the pastry around the sausage meat, using a little egg wash to seal the roll. Place the rolls on a non-stick baking sheet. Make three shallow slices, diagonally through the top of pastry just until the sausage meat shows. Brush the top of each roll with egg wash. Bake for 15 to 20 minutes until golden brown.

Scotch Eggs

1 lb sage sausage meat
5 eggs
Plain bread crumbs
Flour
Vegetable oil for deep frying.

Hard boil four of the eggs and allow to cool. Preheat the oven to 375°. Peel the eggs. Make an egg wash with 1 egg and a little water. Roll an egg in the flour and then mold ¼ of the sausage meat around the egg, making sure it is an even thickness all over. Roll the egg, gently in the egg wash, and then coat evenly in bread crumbs. Repeat with the other hard boiled eggs. Deep fry the eggs until brown. Finish cooking in the oven on a baking sheet until the sausage is cooked through. Cool on a wire rack to room temperature.

For lunch: Serve with a salad.
For Dinner: Serve with baked beans and chips.

Steak and Ale Pie

½ (17.5 ounce) package frozen puff pastry, thawed
1 tbsp lard
½ lb cubed steak
¼ lb carrots, diced
¼ lb turnips, diced
½ lb peeled and cubed potatoes
¼ lb onions, diced
2 cups bitter ale
1 tbsp prepared English mustard
1 tbsp cornstarch
¼ cup cold water
½ tbsp marjoram
½ tbsp thyme
salt and pepper to taste

Preheat oven to 375 degrees F (190 degrees C).
Heat a large skillet over high heat. Add lard, then meat. Toss to coat meat, and sauté just long enough to brown meat on all sides. Remove from heat. Place meat in a 1 quart baking dish. Add carrots, turnip, potatoes, and onion. Mix well. Place 1 cup water and ale in a small saucepan. Bring to a simmer. Mix cornstarch with mustard and ¼ cup cold water until smooth. Slowly pour cornstarch mixture into simmering ale mixture, whisking constantly. Continue to simmer until mixture has thickened. Add salt and pepper to taste. Pour mixture over meat and vegetables. Trim puff pastry to fit over top of filling.
Bake in preheated oven for 45 to 50 minutes, until pastry is deep golden brown.

Steak and Kidney Pie

Filling
¼ cup butter
2 ½ lb. sirloin chopped into ½ inch cubes
Salt and pepper
1 onion, chopped
1 lb beef kidney, trimmed of fat and membrane
½ lb. mushrooms, sliced
¼ cup chopped shallots
1 clove garlic, minced
1-½ cups beef stock

1 tsp dried tarragon
1 tsp Worcestershire sauce
1 tsp salt
¼ tsp freshly ground pepper
¾ cup water
2 tbsp flour

Pastry
3 tbsp lard (shortening)
¾ tsp salt
1 cup flour
2 tbsp ice water

Soak kidney in salt water for one hour, drain, and dry on paper towels. Remove the cores from the kidneys and cut into ½ inch cubes. For pastry: Combine flour and salt; cut in lard or shortening until a coarse meal like consistency. Add water; stir just until combined. Form into a ball. Wrap in plastic wrap and chill for 15 minutes. Heat butter in heavy skillet. Sprinkle meat lightly with salt and pepper. Brown beef well on all sides. Push beef to one side; add onion, kidneys, mushrooms, shallots, and garlic. Sauté until golden. Add beef stock, tarragon, Worcestershire sauce, salt, pepper. Cover and simmer about 1 hour, or until meat is tender. Combine water and flour; stir in; cook and stir until thickened. Put meat mixture into a 2-quart casserole; cool to lukewarm. Roll pastry to 1-inch larger than casserole. Place on top of meat mixture. Trim; seal edge. Cut a small hole in center of pastry. Bake at 450 degrees for 15 minutes; reduce heat to 375 degrees and bake 20 minutes more or until crust is golden and filling is bubbly.

Toad in the Hole

1 batch of Yorkshire Pudding
6 bratwurst or plain pork sausages

Prepare the Yorkshire Pudding batter as usual. While the batter is resting, pan fry the sausages will they are well browned and cooked through.

When the batter has rested, and the baking dish and oil are hot, pour the batter in the baking dish, place the sausages arranged evenly on the top and bake according to the directions for the Yorkshire Pudding.

In the pan you cooked the sausages in, add two tbsp of flour and 1 heaping tbsp of beef glaze, stirring until the flour has cooked slightly to remove the floury flavor. Remove the pan from the heat and add water slowly at first, stirring constantly to avoid lumps. Gradually add enough water to make about 1 pint of gravy. Return to the heat and simmer for about 10 minutes, stirring occasionally. If the mixture is too thick, thin with water and bring back to temperature. Season to taste.

Serve with the gravy, carrots, and peas.

Welsh Rarebit

1 tbsp butter
4 oz grated cheddar cheese
1 tsp prepared English mustard
2 tbsp real ale
3 slices of toast

Melt the butter in a small pan. Mix the remaining ingredients into the melted butter, and cook very gently until smooth and creamy. Spread on the hot toast and brown lightly under the broiler. Serve immediately.

Beef Olives

1 lb flank steak
3 cups bread crumbs
8 tbsp chopped parsley
6 oz butter
4 anchovy filets
4 tsp lemon juice
2 eggs
½ cup flour
2 shallots finely chopped
20 oz beef stock

Preheat the oven to 325°F.

Cut the meat into thin slices, about 3 inches long by 1½ inches wide. Make a stuffing from the bread crumbs, parsley, butter, egg, lemon juice, anchovies, salt and pepper. Place about ¼ cup of the stuffing on one end of a piece of beef, roll the beef around the stuffing, and tie at both ends with string.

In a large, cast iron pan, melt about ¼ cup of lard and brown the beef rolls turning often to get them well browned all over. Remove the rolls from the pan. Sauté the shallots in the same pan until they are soft, add the flour, and stir till the mixture is bubbly and the floury flavor is gone – this should take about 1 minute over medium heat. Remove the pan from the heat and whisk in a little of the stock to make a thick paste. Gradually whisk in the remainder of the stock over the heat. Add the beef rolls back to the pan and place in the oven for an hour or until the beef is tender.

Beef Croquettes

4 cups ground left-over roast beef
1 cup cold mashed potato
2 tbsp minced parsley
2 eggs
1 onion
Bread crumbs
Vegetable oil for frying
½ tsp Salt
½ tsp black pepper
¼ cup gravy

Combine the mashed potato, parsley, 2 tbsp onion juice, salt and pepper. Mix in the ground, left-over roast beef, the egg to bind the mixture, and a little gravy to moisten. Form the mixture into cakes, dip into a beaten egg, and then into breadcrumbs to coat. Fry over medium low heat until golden brown.

Serve with gravy and vegetables.

Ploughman's Lunch

Not so much a recipe as a serving suggestion. This is a country pub staple and offers a tasty, nutritious lunch that in my mind is hard to beat, especially when taken with a pint of real British Ale.

Cheese: All sorts of cheeses are offered these days, but for me, the best is an aged, real Cheddar, a Cheshire or other strong, crumbly cheese. It is often served in very large wedges.

A simple salad: Salad in Britain usually means very simply lettuce and tomato, perhaps radishes, served with Salad Cream; but these days a wide variety of dressings are available.

Crusty, fresh bread, served in ample quantities with good quality butter.

Serve all this with, pickled onions and other pickles and relishes. Real cheddar goes especially well with 'Branford Relish'.

Shepherd's Pie

Shepherd's pie is the way to use left over roast lamb.

1 lb left over roast lamb
¼ cup drippings from the roast
¼ cup plain flour
Beef stock
1 lb bag frozen mixed peas and carrots
Mashed potato
Salt and pepper

Preheat oven to 350°F.

In a large skillet, melt the dripping and add the flour and cook, while whisking over medium heat. When the mixture is bubbly and beginning change color, remove from the heat, and whisk in a little of the stock to make a thick paste, add ¼ tsp of black pepper. Over the heat, slowly add enough stock to make the gravy. The gravy should be quite thick enough to coat the back of a spoon. Simmer the gravy for about ten minutes, thinning if necessary with a little stock. Meanwhile, grind the lamb in a meat grinder. When the gravy has simmered, add the ground lamb and the frozen vegetables to the gravy and mix well. Put the lamb mixture into the bottom of a large, deep casserole. Over the top of the meat, spread a two inch thick layer of mashed potato over the top. Bake in the preheated oven for 30 minutes or until the top is golden brown and the filling bubbly.

Cottage Pie is made in just the same way, but using left-over roast beef. A quick version of Cottage Pie can be made using browned, ground beef.

Fisherman's Pie

A traditional Scottish recipe

1¼ lb cooked white fish
3 tbsp flour
3 tbsp butter
1 pint milk
¼ tsp salt
¼ tsp white pepper
1 lb Mash (whipped potato)
2 medium onions finely chopped
1 cup grated cheddar cheese

Preheat oven to 400°F.

Scald milk in a saucepan and set aside. Melt 3 tbsp of butter in a saucepan, and add flour. Cook over low heat for 3 – 4 minutes, whisking constantly until no floury flavor remains but the mixture has not begun to change color. Slowly drizzle in the milk, while whisking. Add the salt and white pepper. Continue cooking slowly until thickened.

Sauté the onions until softened and translucent, remove from the heat. Flake the white fish into the onions, add the white sauce, and mix well, but not so much as to break up the fish too much.

Put the fish mixture in the bottom of a deep, buttered casserole. Layer the mashed potato over the fish mixture, dot with butter and sprinkle the cheese over the top.

Bake until the top is golden brown.

Serve with green vegetables.

Bangers and Mash

Again, more of a serving suggestion than a recipe, but a traditional pub item.

You will need:
    Bangers (sausages)
    Mash (mashed potatoes)

Pan fry the bangers and serve with a generous dollop of mash and green peas with gravy over bangers and mash.

Side Dishes

Recipes

- Chips 39
- Real Gravy 40
- Roast Potatoes 41
- Soda Bread 42
- Yorkshire Pudding 43
- Cauliflower Cheese 44
- Mushy Peas 45
- Mash 46
- Bread Sauce 47

Chips – aka French Fries

1 (8oz) potato per person
Vegetable oil (real chip lovers would fry in lard!)

Heat the oil to 325°F. Peel the potatoes and slice them into thick slices. Cut the slices into the size chips you want. Place the chips in a kitchen towel and make sure they are quite dry. Put the chips into the hot oil and fry for about 5 minutes. Remove the chips from the oil, letting as much oil as possible drip back into the pan and place the chips on paper towels. Turn the heat up so that the oil reaches 375°F. Refry the chips until they are golden and crispy. Drain again, and place on paper towels and salt immediately so that the salt melts onto the chips. Serve immediately.

Real Gravy

¼ cup lard
¼ cup bacon drippings
½ cup plain flour
1 tbsp beef base
½ tsp black pepper
Salt
Water

In a large saucepan, melt the lard and drippings. When hot, add the flour, and beef base to the pan and whisk, over medium heat, until the mixture is bubbly. Remove from the heat and gradually whisk in a little water to make a thick, lump free paste. Return to the heat and immediately add water while whisking vigorously to a little thinner than you wish to serve the gravy. Add the pepper and allow the gravy to simmer for 10 minutes, whisking often. Adjust the seasoning to taste.

Roast Potatoes

Potatoes - *about 7oz per person*
Lard
Salt

Put the fat about quarter of an inch deep in a heavy metal roasting pan, - make sure the pan is big enough to hold the potatoes in a well-spaced single layer, and heavy enough to go on the range - and place the pan in the oven at 375F for 20 minutes, to get hot.

Peel the potatoes, and cut them into quarters lengthwise. Place them into a large pan of boiling, salted water and cook for 10 minutes. Drain them in a colander, cover with a towel and leave to dry for five minutes. Give the colander a good shake to rough up the surface of the potatoes.

Lift the roasting pan on to the range and heat the fat until bubbly. Spoon the potatoes in carefully – they will splatter. Turn them in the fat then return to the oven (top shelf) for 15 minutes. Turn again, using a flat spatula or fish slice, then roast for another 15 minutes or so, until golden. Place on to a serving dish, salt, and serve immediately.

Soda Bread

4 cups plain flour
1 tsp salt
1 tsp baking soda
1 tsp sugar (optional)
2 cups buttermilk

Preheat the oven to 450°F. Sieve the dry ingredients together into a large bowl. Scoop up handfuls and allow to drop back into the bowl to aerate the mixture. Add enough buttermilk to make a soft dough. Working as quickly as possible as the buttermilk and soda are already reacting, knead the dough lightly – too much will toughen it and too little means it will not rise properly.

Form a round loaf about as thick as your fist. Place the loaf on a lightly floured baking sheet, and score a cross in the top with a floured knife. Place at once in the oven and bake for 30-35 minutes. When fully baked, the loaf should sound hollow when rapped on the bottom. Wrap immediately in a clean towel to keep the crust from hardening too much.

Yorkshire Pudding

1⅓ cups milk
4 eggs
½ tsp salt
1⅔ cups all purpose flour
⅛ cup of vegetable oil

Whisk together the milk, eggs and salt and let it stand for 15 minutes. Preheat the oven to 425°F. pour the oil into a baking 13x9" baking dish and put in the oven. Whisk in the flour and let stand for a further 15 minutes.

Pour the batter into the preheated baking dish and bake for 15 to 20 minutes until it has raised and is golden brown all over.

Cauliflower Cheese

1 large cauliflower
1¼ cups milk
8 oz good Cheddar Cheese
3 tbsp plain flour
3 tbsp butter
½ cup fresh breadcrumbs
½ tsp dried English mustard
¼ tsp nutmeg
Dash of cayenne pepper
Salt and black pepper

Pre-heat oven to 450°F.
Trim the cauliflower & break into small florets.
Boil in salted water for 10-15 minutes or until just tender.
Drain in a colander and then place in a buttered ovenproof baking dish.

Add flour and butter to a saucepan. Cook until bubbly and there is no floury flavor, about 1 minute. Whisking continuously add the milk slowly and heat until the sauce thickens, boils and is smooth. Allow to simmer for a further 2 minutes. Add three-quarters of the grated cheese, mustard, nutmeg, cayenne and seasoning. Cook for further minute stirring well. Pour the sauce over the cauliflower. Mix the remaining cheese, and breadcrumbs together, sprinkle over the top. Bake in the oven for about 15 to 25 minutes until golden brown and bubbling.

Mushy Peas

Mushy peas are often served with fish and chips.

1 (10 ounce) package frozen green peas
¼ cup heavy cream
1 tbsp butter
½ teaspoon salt
½ teaspoon freshly ground black pepper

Bring a shallow pot of lightly salted water to a boil over medium-high heat. Add frozen peas, and cook for 3 minutes, or until tender.

Drain peas, and transfer to a blender or large food processor. Add cream, butter, salt and pepper to peas, and process until blended, but still thick with small pieces of peas. Adjust seasonings to taste, and serve immediately.

Mash (mashed or whipped potatoes)

6 large potatoes
1 cup whipping cream
½ cup salted butter
Salt and white pepper to taste.

Peel the potatoes and cube them into equally sized cubes (about 1 inch square). Rinse the potatoes under cold water.

Boil the potatoes in plenty of lightly salted water for 15 to 20 minutes or until the point of a knife meets no resistance when inserted. Drain the water from the potatoes – reserve the water if you want to make pan gravy, it thickens beautifully.

To whip the potatoes:- Add the butter in a lump to the potatoes and put a lid on the pan, and leave for 5 minutes. Add the cream, and seasonings and use an electric hand mixer to whip the potatoes until smooth and creamy.

To mash the potatoes:- Add the butter, cream and seasonings to the potatoes and use a potato masher to evenly mash.

Adjust seasoning to taste.

Bread Sauce

4 oz fresh white breadcrumbs
1 large onion
20 whole cloves
2 bay leaves
10 black peppercorns
1¼ pints milk
2 oz butter
2 tbsp cream
Salt
Black pepper

Cut the onion in half and stick the cloves in it. Place the onion, studded with cloves, the bay leaf and peppercorns, in a saucepan together with the milk. Add some salt then bring everything up to boil. Remove from the heat, cover the pan and leave in a warm place for the milk to infuse for two hours or more.

Remove the onion, bay leaf and peppercorns and keep them on one side. Stir the breadcrumbs into the milk and add 1 oz of the butter. Leave the saucepan on a very low heat, stirring occasionally, until the crumbs have swollen and thickened the sauce, about 15 minutes. Now replace the clove-studded onion, the bay leaf and the peppercorns and again leave the pan in a warm place until the sauce is needed.

Just before serving, remove the onion and spices. Reheat gently then beat in the remaining butter and the cream and taste to check the seasoning.

Serve as a sauce along side any roast bird

Puddings

Recipes

Apricot Fool 51
Rice Pudding 52
Sticky Toffee Pudding 53
Trifle 54
Baked Apples 55
Blackberry Pie 56
Cherry Bakewell Tart 57

Apricot Fool

1 pound fresh apricots
Sugar
10 oz whipping cream

Bake the apricots in a gentle oven (with the pits in) in a little water and sugar until they are soft. When cooked, de-pit the apricots, mash them to a puree, allow to cool. Whip the cream to stiff peaks and mix the apricots into the cream. Sweeten a little if needed, but leave fairly tart. Serve chilled.

Rice Pudding

2 cups cooked white rice
2 cups whole milk
1¼ cup cream
¼ cup sugar
⅛ tsp ground nutmeg

In a large nonstick sauté pan over medium heat, combine the cooked rice and milk. Heat until the mixture begins to boil. Decrease the heat to low and cook at a simmer until the mixture begins to thicken, stirring frequently, approximately 5 minutes.

Increase the heat to medium, add the cream, sugar, and nutmeg and continue to cook until the mixture just begins to thicken again, approximately 8 minutes. When the rice just begins to thicken, remove from the heat. Transfer the mixture to a glass bowl and place plastic wrap directly on the surface of the pudding. Serve chilled or at room temperature.

For the school-boy adaptation of this, serve warm and stir in a spoonful of strawberry jam.

Sticky Toffee Pudding

2 sticks unsalted butter, softened
1 cup self-rising cake flour
1 cup pitted chopped dates
1¼ cups packed dark brown sugar
1 large egg

Put oven rack in middle position and preheat oven to 350°F. Butter and flour an 8- by 2-inch round cake pan.

Simmer dates in ½ cup brandy and ½ cup water in a 1-quart heavy saucepan, covered, until soft, about 5 minutes. Let stand, covered.

Beat together 1 stick butter and ¼ cup brown sugar in a large bowl until light and fluffy.

Beat in egg until combined. Add flour and ⅛ tsp salt and mix until just combined. Drain the dates and mix until just combined well.

Pour batter into pan and bake until a wooden pick or skewer inserted in center comes out clean, about 30 minutes.

Meanwhile, melt remaining stick butter in a 2-quart heavy saucepan over moderate heat and stir in remaining cup brown sugar, ⅓ cup water, and a pinch of salt. Boil over moderately high heat, uncovered, stirring occasionally, until sugar is dissolved and sauce is reduced to about 1¼ cups, about 6 minutes. Remove from heat and cover.

Transfer pudding in pan to a rack and poke holes all over at 1-inch intervals with a chopstick. Gradually pour half of warm sauce evenly over hot pudding. Let stand until almost all of sauce is absorbed, about 20 minutes.

Run a knife around edge of pan to loosen. Invert a plate over pudding and invert pudding onto plate. Pour remaining warm sauce over pudding and serve immediately.

Trifle

Ladyfingers
Sweet Marsala wine
Strawberry or Raspberry Jello
2 cups milk
¼ cup cornstarch
3 eggs
⅛ tsp vanilla extract
1 cup whipping cream
¼ cup confectioner's sugar
Confectioner's sprinkles

Place ladyfingers in bottom of a large glass bowl suitable for serving from. Pour enough Marsala over to soak the ladyfingers. Make the Jello according to the directions on the package and pour over the ladyfingers. Allow the Jello to set. Meanwhile, make the custard – Scald 1 ½ cups of milk; blend the remaining milk with ¼ cup of cornstarch. Mix sugar and salt into hot milk, and blend in cornstarch paste. Heat over direct, moderate heat, stirring constantly until the mixture thickens. Mix a little of the hot mixture into three lightly beaten eggs. Place hot mixture in a double boiler over simmering water, and add the tempered eggs. Heat, stirring constantly for 2-3 minutes until thick and no flavor of raw egg remains. Mix in vanilla extract. Allow to cool until just warm and pour over Jello in bowl. Allow to cool completely in the refrigerator. Before serving, whip cream and confectioners sugar to a stiff peak, and spread over custard. Sprinkle top with colored sprinkles.

Baked Apples

Granny Smith apples
Raisins
Brown sugar
Butter
Cane sugar

Preheat the oven to 375°F

Core the apples, and trim the bottom (stem end) ½" inch from the cores. Score a shallow line around the waist of the apple with a sharp pairing knife. Reinsert the bottom of the core into the apple. Place the apples on a buttered baking dish. Fill the cored apple with a mixture of mostly raisins and a little butter and sugar. Bake for 30 – 40 minutes or until tender but not mushy.

Serve warm with vanilla ice-cream, or if you can find it, Golden Syrup, made by Tate and Lyle in England, drizzled over.

Blackberry Pie

4 cups fresh blackberries
½ cup white sugar
½ cup all-purpose flour
1 recipe pastry for a 9 inch double crust pie
2 tbsp milk
½ cup sugar

Combine 3½ cups berries with the sugar and flour. Spoon the mixture into an unbaked pie shell. Spread the remaining ½ cup berries on top of the sweetened berries, and cover with the top crust. Seal and crimp the edges. Brush the top crust with milk, and sprinkle with ¼ cup sugar.
Bake at 425°F for 15 minutes. Reduce the temperature of the oven to 375°F, and bake for an additional 20 to 25 minutes.

Serve with whipping cream or vanilla ice-cream.

Cherry Bakewell Tart

A wonderful, traditional English desert.

1 batch Shortcrust Pastry

Filling
Cherry preserve
¼ lb butter
¼ lb sugar
¼ lb ground almonds
2 eggs well beaten
A few drops Almond extract

Preheat oven to 375°F.

Line a shallow pie pan with pastry and spread a thick layer of cherry preserve in the bottom.

Cream together the sugar and butter, and then mix in all the other ingredients, and spread over the jam.

Bake for 25 – 30 minutes until the filling is set.

Option: Some Bakewells come iced. See recipe in 'Basics'. Spread the icing over the top of the cooled tart.

The Basics

Recipes

Shortcrust Pastry 61
Flaky Pastry 62
Bangers 63
Glacé Icing 64

Shortcrust Pastry

Enough for a single pie crust.

4 cups plain flour
¼ lb each of butter and lard
2 scant tbsp confectioner's sugar
½ tsp salt
Cold water

Sift flour, sugar, and salt together into a large bowl. Rub in the butter and lard until the mixture is crumbly. Using as little water as possible, mix into a firm dough. Form the dough into a ball. Wrap in foil and leave in the refrigerator for at least an hour. Roll out the dough on a floured surface for use.

Flaky Pastry

Enough for a double pie crust

2½ cups flour
1 tsp salt
⅔ cup vegetable shortening, chilled
½ cup ice water

Sift the flour and salt into a large bowl. Cut in shortening with a pastry blender until the mixture resembles coarse meal. Sprinkle water over the surface, 1 tbsp at a time, and mix lightly and quickly with a fork, until the pastry just holds together. Shape the dough into a ball on a floured surface. Divide the dough into two equal portions. Using a floured rolling pin, roll out one portion of the dough into a circle a couple of inches larger than the pie plate you intend to use. Lay the rolling pin over the center of the dough, fold the dough in two over the rolling pin and use the pin to lift the dough over the pie plate. Mold the dough to the plate, filling any crack with pieces of moistened dough, and trimming the edge with a sharp knife. Roll out the second portion of dough slightly larger than the pie plate. Fill the pie, and moisten the rim of the pie with a little water on a pastry brush. Place the lid over the filling. Trim the overhanging pastry and crimp the edge closed with the tines of a fork. Cut three slightly v-shaped slits in the top of the pie for it to vent. Bake as directed.

Bangers

1 lb fatty pork
½ cup fresh breadcrumbs
2 egg yolks
½ tsp nutmeg
½ tsp ground cloves
½ tsp mace
1 tsp thyme
Salt
Pepper
Sausage skins (optional)

Pass the pork through the fine blade of a meat grinder at least twice. Mix all the ingredients together in a bowl. If you have a sausage maker, fill the casings immediately with the mixture, tying off at about 4-5 inch intervals – this process can be done with a funnel and handle of a wooden spoon but it is laborious. If you do not want to make a cased sausage, chill the mixture off slightly in a refrigerator and form into sausage shapes or patties, and flour the outside lightly before pan frying.

Glacé Icing

2 cups sifted confectioner's sugar
2 tbsp corn syrup
2 tbsp water

Place all the ingredients in the top of a double boiler over simmering water and heat, stirring, until the sugar dissolves and the mixture is smooth. Do not allow the water beneath to boil or the icing will be granular.

Index

Apricot Fool 51

Baked Apples 55

Bangers 63

Bangers and Mash 35

Beef Croquettes 31

Beef in Guinness 16

Beef Olives 30

Blackberry Pie 56

Branford Relish 7

Bread Sauce 47

Cauliflower Cheese 44

Cherry Bakewell Tart 57

Cheshire Pork and Apple Pie 15

Chips 39

Cornish Pasties 17

Cottage Pie *(see Shepherd's Pie)*

Farmhouse Pie 18

Fish and Chips 19

Fisherman's Pie 34

Flaky Pastry 62

Gammon Steaks 20

Glacé Icing 64

Green Tomato Chutney 8

Mash 46

Mushy Peas 45

Piccalilli 9

Pickled Onions 10

Ploughman's Lunch 32

Pork Pie 21

Real Gravy 40

Rice Pudding 52

Roast Beef 23

Roast Potatoes 41

Salad Cream 11

Sausage Rolls 24

Scotch Eggs 25

Shepherd's Pie *and Cottage Pie* 33

Shortcrust Pastry 61

Soda Bread 42

Steak and Ale Pie 26

Steak and Kidney Pie 27

Sticky Toffee Pudding 53

Toad in the Hole 28

Trifle 54

Welsh Rarebit 29

Yorkshire Pudding 43

Made in the USA
Lexington, KY
01 December 2011